Contents

Social Studies

And more...

We're on Our Way!

Help the Romeros and their friends get to the zoo.
Look at the names of places they will pass.
Number the words in ABC order.
Then follow the path from 1 to 8.

HOSPITAL

GROCERY

FIRE STATION

BANK

Try This!

Draw a map. Show how to get from your house to a
favourite place. Show the streets on which you travel.
Include the places you pass.

Alphabetising/Interpreting a Map

Which animal knows its ABCs?

The alpha-bat!

3

Alphabetising/Interpreting a Map

What's Up at the Zoo?

Look at the zoo map and the map key.
Then follow the directions.

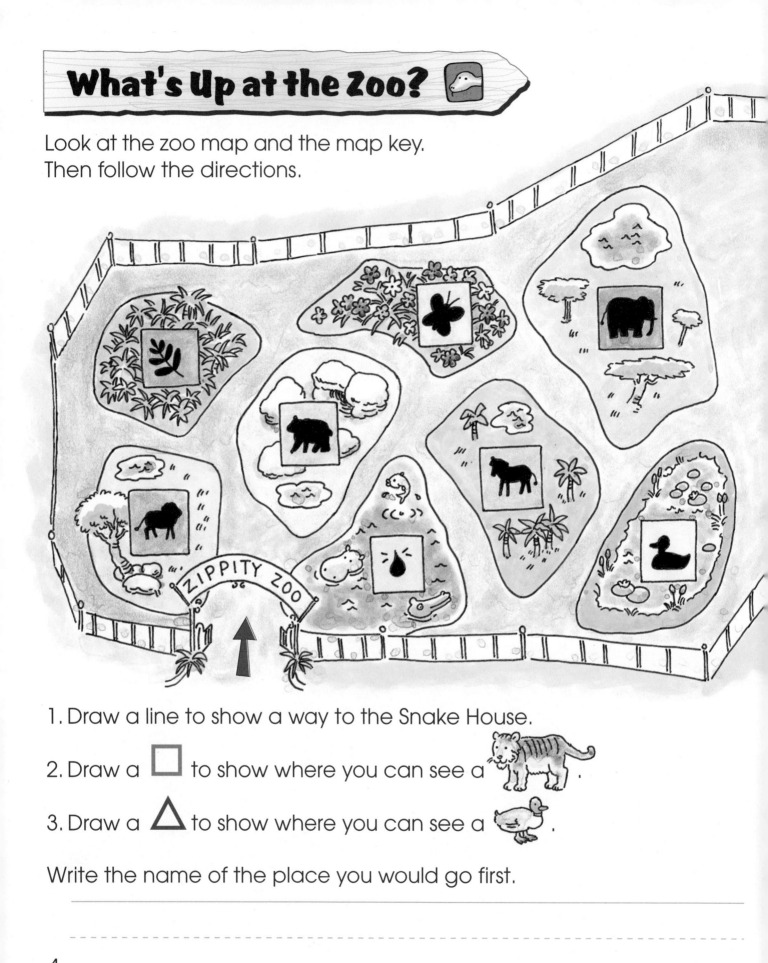

1. Draw a line to show a way to the Snake House.

2. Draw a ☐ to show where you can see a 🐯 .

3. Draw a △ to show where you can see a 🦆 .

Write the name of the place you would go first.

_____

_____

4. _____

Using a Map and Map Key

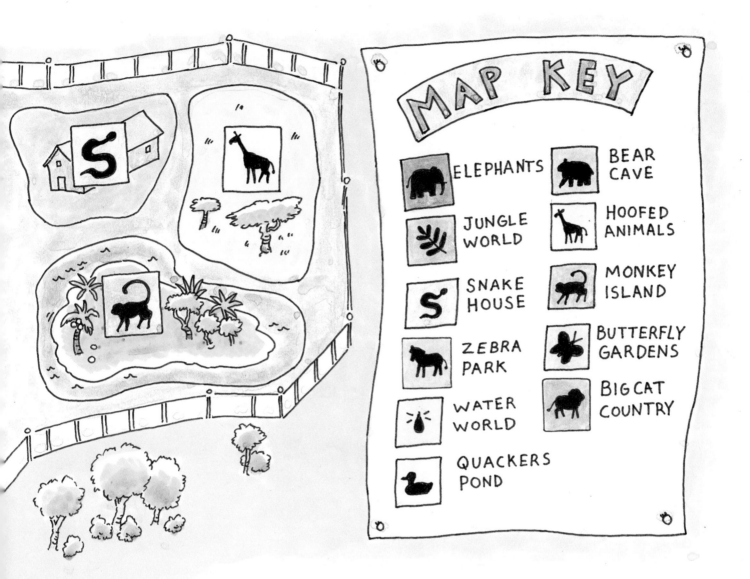

Write **yes** or **no**.

5. Can you see an  in the zoo? _____

6. Can you see a in the zoo? _____

7. Can you see a in the zoo? _____

5

Puzzling Names

Write the first letter of each picture.
Read the animal name.
Write the number in its circle.

_____ _____ _____ _____

1. _____

_____ _____ _____ _____ _____ _____

2. _____

_____ _____ _____ _____ _____

3. _____

Try This!

Make a puzzle! You need nature magazines to cut up,
scissors, glue and heavy paper or cardboard.
1. Cut out a large picture of an animal.
2. Glue the picture on cardboard or heavy paper.
3. Cut the picture into puzzle pieces.
4. Put your puzzle back together.

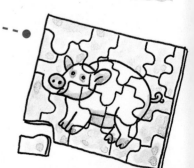

Phonics – Initial Consonants

Water World

Say **a**, **e**, **i**, **o** and **u**. These are the long vowels.
Then say the words on the fish.
Colour the long vowel fish **orange**.

The other words have short vowel sounds.
Colour the short vowel fish **green**.

Help the squid get to her cave.
Draw a line to connect the long vowel fish.

bat

fish

fin

me

hot

boat

crab

ten

bite

Whale

huge

swim

sea

home

Phonics – Vowels

Honey Bear

Honey Bear is running in circles!
She is looking for words with short vowel sounds.
Start at the arrow. Write eight words you find.
Then go the other way. Say the words.

_____

1. _____

2. _____

3. _____

4. _____

5. _____

6. _____

7. _____

8. _____

Try This!

Have an adult help you make this honey of a treat.

2 apples, cored & peeled	1/2 cup walnut pieces
1/2 cup raisins	1/4 cup apple juice
1 tablespoon honey	8 digestive biscuits

1. Chop the apples, walnuts and raisins.
2. Stir in the juice and honey.
3. Spread on digestive biscuits. Eat!

Phonics – Short Vowels

A Cool Rhyme

Read the rhyme.
Then draw a line under each number word.

Penguin Pals

Five little penguin pals resting on the shore

One took a dip, and then there were four

Four little penguin pals walking by the sea

One little slip, and then there were three

Three little penguin pals with nothing to do

One little trip, and then there were two

Two little penguin pals looking for fun

One little flip, and then there was one

One little penguin all alone

He jumped in too, and now there are none!

Write the words that rhyme with **tip**.
Say other words that rhyme with **tip**.

1. _____   2. _____

3. _____   4. _____

Rhyming Words/Number Words

Quackers Pond

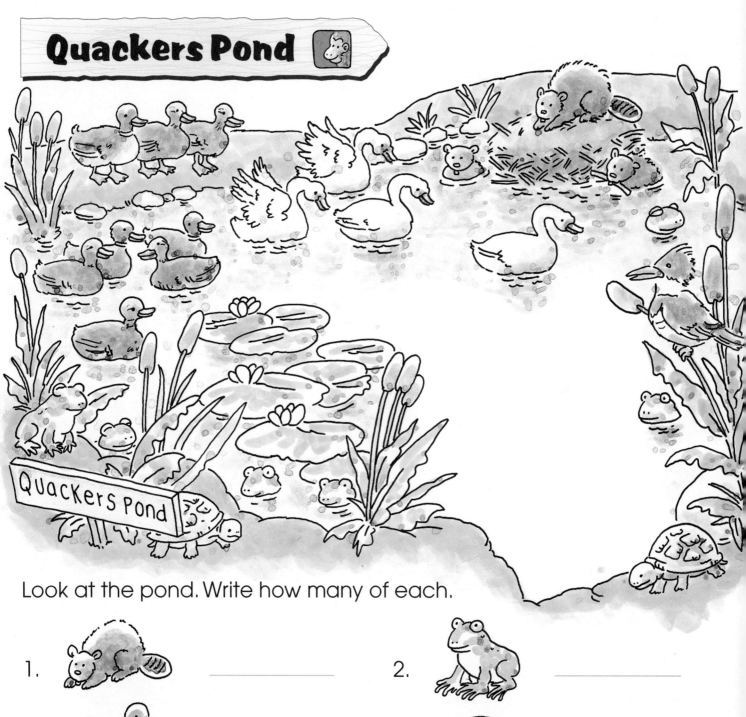

Look at the pond. Write how many of each.

1. _____

2. _____

3.  _____

4. _____

5. _____

6. _____

7. Draw 10 in the pond.

Counting to Ten

Sneaky Snakes

Write an **s** blend to finish each picture name. Choose from these.

st · sn · sl · sk · sp · sw

1. _____ ake

2. _____ an

3. _____ ider

4. _____ unk

5. _____ ug

6. _____ arfish

Circle words with **s** blends in the puzzle.

x	b	s	k	u	n	k
v	s	t	o	p	s	g
s	w	a	n	g	n	s
f	t	r	y	c	o	l
t	u	f	z	j	w	u
s	p	i	d	e	r	g
y	o	s	n	a	k	e
p	q	h	s	n	a	p

Try This!

Play a blend game. You need six paper cups and a pen. Label each cup with one blend: sn, sl, st, sp, sw, sk. Line up the cups on a table. Toss a soft ball or beanbag toy at the cups. For each cup you knock over, say a word that begins with the blend.

Phonics – **S** Blends

Desert Trail

Follow the path through the desert.
Add numerals to write the **sums**.
Subtract numerals to write the **differences**.

Addition and Subtraction

Where Are the Animals?

Where are the animals on the Desert Trail?
Finish each sentence with a word below.

over   **under**   in   **across**   on

1. The roadrunner  runs <u>under</u> the .

2. The lizard  sleeps _____ the .

3. The jackrabbit  leaps _____ the .

4. The snake  glides _____ the .

5. The owl sits _____ the .

Play a game of Simon Says with family members or friends. Use the words from the oval on this page as you play.

Positional Prepositions

We Work at the Zoo

Here are four people who work at Zippity Zoo.
Circle the name in each sentence.

Remember – a person's name begins with a capital letter.

Jan helps sick animals.　　　Bob keeps animal homes clean.

Chan teaches sea animals.　　Lisa feeds hungry animals.

Write the correct name under each picture.

1. _____　　2. _____

3. _____　　4. _____

The names of special places begin with capital letters.
Zippity Zoo is a special place.
Zippity and **Zoo** begin with capital letters.
Circle the name of the special place in each sentence.

1. Parrots  live in Jungle World .

2. Ducks  swim in Quackers Pond .

3. Deer run in Zebra Park .

4. Monkeys make noise on Monkey Island .

Look back at pages 4 and 5. Write the name of the
special place bears live.

Big Cat Country

A word can name one. **lion**

A word can name more than one. **lions**

Many words add **s** to name more than one.

Write a number sentence about each picture.
Add **s** to make the name of each kind of cat mean more than one.

+ _____

= _____ tiger _____ .

+ _____

= _____ leopard _____ .

+ _____

= _____ bobcat _____ .

+ _____

= _____ lion _____ .

Plural Nouns/Addition Facts

Disappearing Animals

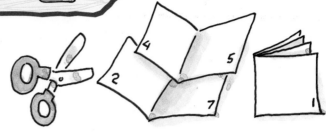

Cut out the book and put it together.
Write number sentences.
Tell the story in your own words.

− _____ = _____

8 _____

Captain Croc's Zippity Zoo Riverboat by

_____

_____

Captain Croc has a riverboat. Animals like to ride in his boat. Here come some now! Turn the page to begin the story.

1

+ _____ = _____

6 _____

− _____ = _____

3 _____

Try This!

Make number sentences using dominoes.
You need a set of dominoes, paper and a pencil.
Look at the number of dots on both halves of
a domino. Write a number sentence to show how
many dots all together.

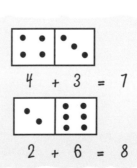

4 + 3 = 7

2 + 6 = 8

Addition and Subtraction Story Problems

Disappearing Animals

**What did the maths book say
to the storybook?**

I've got a lot of problems!

2 _____ + _____ = _____

_____ − _____ = _____ 7

4 _____ + _____ = _____

_____ − _____ = _____ 5

Try This!

1	2	3	4
5	6	7	8
9	10	11	12

Make this game board. You need a large piece of paper, chalk, and coins, buttons or stones. Use the chalk to make the game board inside on the paper or outside on the pavement. Toss two coins or buttons on a paper game board or two stones on a large chalk game board. Subtract the smaller number from the larger number.

Addition and Subtraction Story Problems

Play Like the Animals

Action words tell what people and animals do.
Under each picture, write an action word from the oval.
Then draw lines to match the children with the
animals doing the same actions.

climb   dig   **slide**   jump

1. _____

2. _____

3. _____

4. _____

19

Verbs

Baby Talk

Some baby animals have names that are different from their parents. A baby pig is a **piglet**. What is a baby cat?

Draw a line from each baby to its parent.

calf

lamb

gosling

pup

fawn

cub

Write a baby animal name to finish each sentence.

_____

_____

1. **Seal** goes with _____ .   2. **Tiger** goes with _____ .

20

Animal Names

Let Me Out!

Some animals hatch from eggs.
Look at these eggs.
Write the name of each animal.

fish   snake
chick   robin

I sing in spring!

1. _____

I love water.

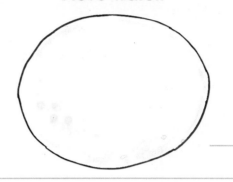

2. _____

I say sssss.

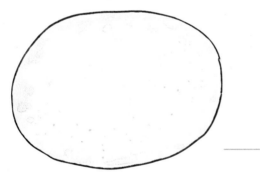

3. _____

I'm yellow.

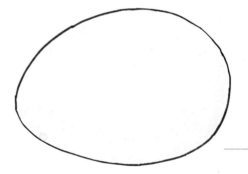

4. _____

Hold the page up to a light or window.
Take a peek inside each egg.
Put a ✓ by the eggs you guessed correctly.

Try This!

Fill a jar with lollies, cotton balls or marbles. Ask family members to guess how many are in the jar. Write down their guesses. Take a guess yourself. Then count the number. Whose guess was closest?

Predicting

Let Me Out!

Were your guesses correct?
Write the animals you got wrong.

fish   snake

chick   robin

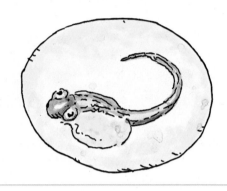

_____

- -

_____

_____

- -

_____

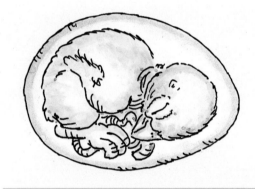

_____

- -

_____

_____

- -

_____

Try This!

Animals use many different things to build their nests.
You can build a nest, too. You need twigs, sticks, feathers,
string, grass and plastic eggs.
1. Weave small sticks and twigs together to make a bowl-shaped nest.
2. Line the nest with soft things like feathers, bits of string and grass.
3. Put the plastic eggs inside your nest.

Hiding Places

A contraction is two words put together to make one word.
A letter or letters is left out.
An apostrophe (') takes the place of the missing letter or letters.

are not ⟶ are n t ⟶ aren't

Circle the contraction in each sentence.
Then circle the animals in the jungle.

Draw a line from each contraction
to the words that form it.

1. can't	Where is
2. Let's	can not
3. Where's	is not
4. isn't	Let us

Contractions/Animal Camouflage

What's Happening This Week?

Read the zoo calendar.

Sunday	Monday	Tuesday	Wednesday	Thursday	Friday	Saturday
Sheep Shearing	Birthday Party for Coco the Camel	Storytime Safari	The Zoo Is for You Day!	Jungle Day Walk	Desert Trail Hike	Spring Egg Hunt

Write the day when these things happen.

1. _____

2. _____

3. _____

4. _____

Sheep Shearing Today!

Write a number sentence about each picture.

1. _____ + _____ = _____

2. _____ − _____ = _____

3. _____ + _____ = _____

4. _____ − _____ = _____

5. _____ + _____ = _____

6. _____ − _____ = _____

Addition and Subtraction Facts

Describe It!

Describing words tell about naming words.

    The **huge** lion roared.

Which word tells about, or **describes**, the lion?

Some describing words tell how animals look or feel.

Write words that tell about the animals.

long   tall   **tiny**   wet   **sleepy**   huge

1. _____

2. _____

3. _____

4. _____

5. _____

6. _____

Adjectives

What a Shape!

Draw an alligator.
Follow these steps.

1.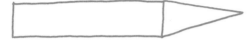

2. Add.

3. Add.

4. Add.

Draw a tiger.
Follow these steps.

1.

2. Add.

3. Add.

4. Add.

1. How many △s
   in step 4?

2. How many ○s
   in step 4?

Think of an animal. Make up a riddle about it. Tell how the animal
looks, feels and sounds.
Example: I'm thinking of a small bird with a red head. It makes
a rat-tat-tat noise. What is it? (A woodpecker)

Monkey Business

Toss a coin on the page. Read the word closest to the coin. Write the word on the chart next to the word that means the same or opposite. Play until the chart is filled.

tall

fast

small

loud

happy

	Same	Opposite
glad		
noisy		
little		
quick		

sad

quiet

big

slow

short

Try This!

Copy the words from the leaves on ten cards. Turn the cards face down to play a game. Turn over two cards at a time. If the words mean the opposite, set the pair aside. If not, turn them face down again. Play until you have matched all the words.

Synonyms and Antonyms

Big Meets Little

Read the names of the big and little animals.
Add two more names to the chart.

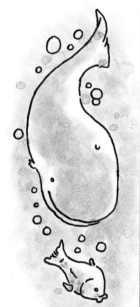

Big animals	Little animals
hippo	chipmunk
elephant	butterfly
giraffe	chick

Plan a story about two animals. Write your ideas.

Which big and little animals meet?

_____

_____

Where do they meet?

_____

_____

What is their problem?

_____

_____

How is the problem solved?

_____

_____

Animal Sizes/Story Structure

Little Weight Watchers

Read the scales.

Colour in the boxes to show how many kilograms each animal weighs.

	1	2	3	4	5	6	7	8	9	10
tiger cub										
baby porcupine										
fox										
snowy owl										
fawn										
opossum										
weight in kilograms	1	2	3	4	5	6	7	8	9	10

Bar Graph/Animal Weights

In the Seal Pool

You need 15 coins or buttons. Read the chart to find out how many to put in or take out of the pool.
Then count how many are left. Write the numerals in the chart.

Put in	Take out	How many are left?	Put in	Put in	How many in all?
9	2		9	6	
10	4		2	8	
12	7		6	5	
8	6		7	7	
15	8		8	8	

Try This!

Use the coins or buttons to write as many different maths equations that equal 15 as you can. Then write equations with three numerals that equal 15.
Example: 6 + 3 + 6 = 15

31

Graph/Addition and Subtraction

Zoomobile Tour Game

You need a coin to toss, two buttons for markers and a
sheet of paper and pencil to keep score.
1. Put your button on Start.
2. Toss the coin. If it's heads, move one space.
   If it's tails, move two spaces.
3. Follow the directions on the square on which you land.
   Make a mark on the score sheet for each right answer.
4. The game is over when you reach Finish.
   The most points wins.

Start

Stuck in
the mud.
Lose 2 points

Name it.
4 points

Subtract
it.
11 − 6 = ___
2 points

Name it.
2 points

Name it.
4 points

Name it.
3 points

Finish the
word.
___ OX
1 point

Name it.
2 points

Name it.
4 points

What's
missing?
2, 4, 6, ___, 10.
3 points

Run out
of petro
Lose
3 points

Add it.
8 + 4 = ___
1 point

You're lost.
?, ?, ?, ?
Lose 1 point.

32 Addition and Subtraction/Animal Identification/Phonics

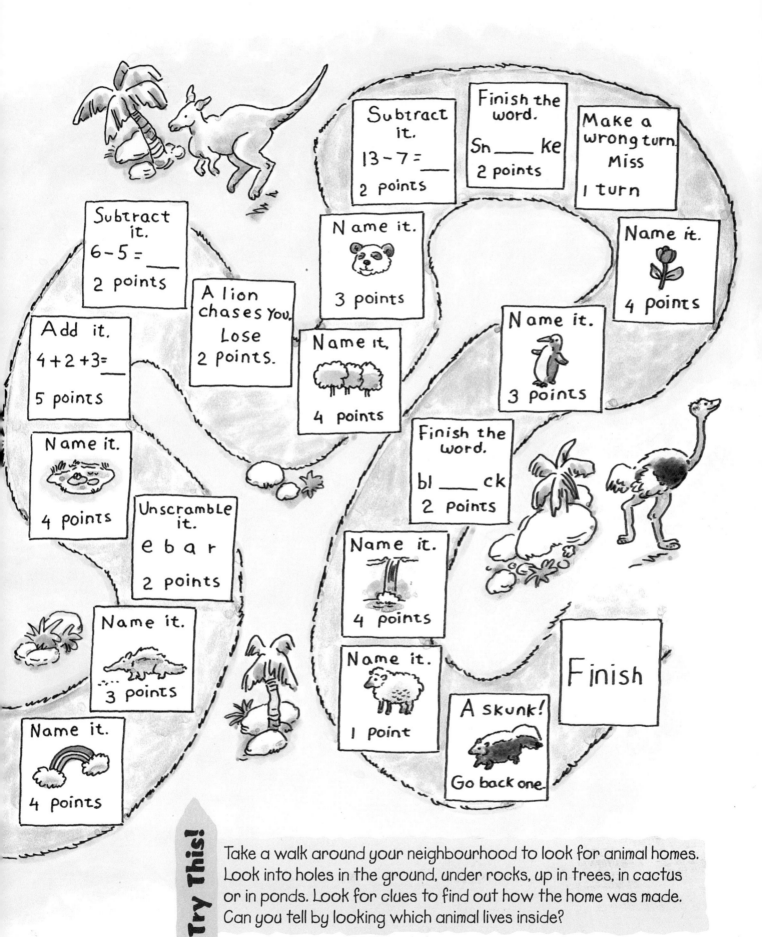

Subtract it.

13 − 7 = ___

2 points

Finish the word.

Sn ___ ke

2 points

Make a wrong turn. Miss 1 turn

Name it.

4 points

Subtract it.

6 − 5 = ___

2 points

A lion chases you. Lose 2 points.

Name it.

3 points

Name it.

4 points

Name it.

3 points

Add it.

4 + 2 + 3 = ___

5 points

Name it.

4 points

Finish the word.

bl ___ ck

2 points

Unscramble it.

e b a r

2 points

Name it.

4 points

Name it.

3 points

Name it.

1 point

A skunk!

Go back one.

Finish

Name it.

4 points

Try This! Take a walk around your neighbourhood to look for animal homes. Look into holes in the ground, under rocks, up in trees, in cactus or in ponds. Look for clues to find out how the home was made. Can you tell by looking which animal lives inside?

Addition and Subtraction/Animal Identification/Phonics

Critter's Cafe

Read the clues. Mark the chart with ✓s.
The first one is done for you.

1. Everyone had fruit.
2. Dad and Ben had a taco.
3. Mum had a salad.

4. Anna had a turkey sandwich.
5. Mum, Ben and Anna had juice.
6. Dad had milk.

	milk	juice	fruit	salad	taco	sandwich
Dad			✓			
Ben			✓			
Mum			✓			
Anna			✓			

Write a person's name under each meal.

1. _____

2. _____

3. _____

4. _____

Make critter place-mats. You need construction paper, crayons or a pen and clear contact paper. Draw animals on the construction paper. Cover with clear contact paper.

Logic/Chart

Start at 2. Connect the dots counting by twos from 2 to 40.

•8   •10

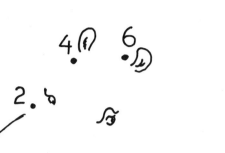

•12

•40   •34   •28   •26   •20   •14

38   36   •32   •30   24   22   18   •16

Read more clues about this animal.
Write the words from the circle in the sentences.

hippo
grass
fat water

1. This animal is very _____ .

2. It spends the day in _____ and eats at night.

3. It can eat 40 kilograms of _____ each night.

4. This animal is a _____ .

Skip Counting by Twos/Animal Characteristics

Who Is Lost?

Dad went to buy popcorn. Now he is lost.
Circle the right answers to help him find the family.

1. Where should Dad walk first?

   to the office   to the water fountain   to the zoo entrance

2. Next, Dad should walk to the ___ .

   flag   rubbish bin   pond

3. Dad will see the family on the bench if he walks by the ___ .

   office   pond   parrot

4. Write **1**, **2**, **3** to show the right order.

   _____ flag   _____ fountain   _____ parrot

5. Draw a red line on the path Dad should take.

36

Map Skills/Reading Comprehension

Ape Escape

Help the ape get to the banana tree.
Count by fives from **5** to **50**.
Colour the squares with these numbers to show the path.

5	10	6	22	13	8
11	15	7	18	31	14
17	20	25	32	47	71
36	22	30	35	40	48
51	56	43	33	45	50

Try This!

Try counting backwards from 50 to 5. Then count by twos from 30 to 2. Count by tens from 100 to 10. How fast can you count?

Skip Counting by Fives

Yipes, Stripes!

Look at each row.
Draw the missing picture to fit the pattern.

1.

2.
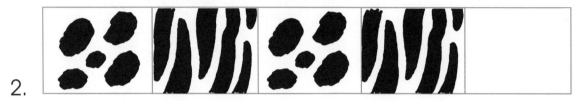

3.

4. Help the tiger get to her cubs. Find the pattern.
   Colour the shapes to finish the path.

Try This!

Collect leaves and flower petals.
Glue them on paper to form
different patterns.

Patterns

Get Out of Here!

Look at each group of animals.
Circle the one that does not belong.
Then draw an animal that belongs.

Forest Theatre

A telling sentence ends with a full stop. (.)
An asking sentence ends with a question mark. (?)

Read the sign. Add a (.) or a (?) in the ◯ at the end of each sentence.

Forest Theatre

1. The theatre is open from 9:00 to 5:00 ◯

2. Have you ever seen an opossum ◯

3. Do you know what a deer eats ◯

4. Come see the show to find out ◯

5. You will meet many forest friends ◯

Declarative and Interrogative Sentences/Punctuation

The Big Screen

Write the letters under the numbers.
The first letter is done for you. Then read each animal name.
Draw a line to match the name to the picture.

1	2	3	4	5	6	7	8	9	10	11	12	13	14	15	16
a	b	c	d	e	i	k	l	m	n	o	p	q	r	s	u

The Stars of the Show

1.
11	12	11	15	15	16	9
o						

2.
4	5	5	14

3.
15	7	16	10	7

4.
15	13	16	6	14	14	5	8

Try This!

Finish this riddle about one of the stars of the show. Write your own words. Ask someone to guess your riddle.

This animal lives in the forest.
Its colour is _____.
It has _____.
What is it?_____.

Using a Number Code/Reading Comprehension

Rise and Shine!

When does each animal get up in the morning?
Write the time.

____ : ____   ____ : ____   ____ : ____

____ : ____   ____ : ____   ____ : ____

Try This!

Ask someone to use a clock with a second hand to time
you. Guess how many numbers you can write in one minute.
Then do it. How close was your guess?

**What do you say to a
clock at noon?**

Hands up!

42

Froggy Grows Up

Look at the pictures.

A   B   C   D   E

Read the sentences.
Write **A**, **B**, **C**, **D** and **E** to show how froggy grows up.

1. _____   Froggy is a tiny tadpole.

2. _____   Froggy is a big frog.

3. _____   Froggy is an egg.

4. _____   Froggy grows four legs.

5. _____   Froggy grows two legs.

Animal Life Cycles

Animal Poll

The zookeeper is counting the animals with hooves.
She needs more animals for the zoo.
Fill in the chart to show how many more she needs.

Kinds of animals		Animals we want	Animals we have	How many more do we need?
camel		8	4	
deer		15	9	
giraffe		10	7	
hippo		12	8	
pig		14	7	
sheep		18	9	
buffalo		9	5	
moose		13	6	

Create your own coin!
1. Cut a large circle from paper or use a white paper plate.
2. Choose an animal for your coin.
3. Draw what your coin will look like.

44

Animal Characteristics/Subtraction Facts/Chart Skills

Who Is Hiding?

One animal with hooves is very shy.
He is hiding behind these numbers.
Find the sums and differences of the numbers in each row.
Then use the code to find out the animal's name.

7	8	9	10	11	12	13	14	15
r	e	s	m	t	o	f	s	v

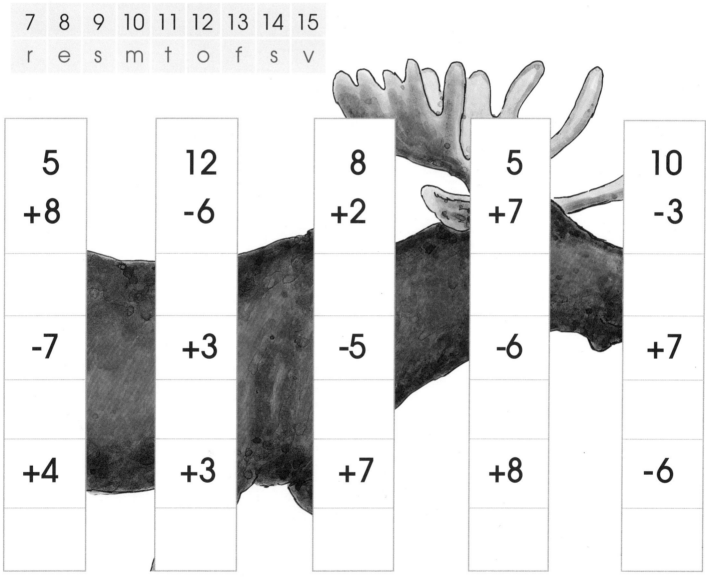

5	12	8	5	10
+8	-6	+2	+7	-3
-7	+3	-5	-6	+7
+4	+3	+7	+8	-6

Look at the last number in each row. Write the letter from
the code box to spell the animal's name.

_____ _____ _____ _____ _____

_____ _____ _____ _____ _____

Addition and Subtraction Facts/Number Code

A Tale of Tracks

Read the story.

Last night we saw some **tracks**. The tracks came from the

forest . They went by the tree . Then they went

down to the pond . We followed the tracks to our

house . What is all that noise? A hungry visitor is eating dinner!

Look at the yard. Follow the tracks.
Number the places from 1 to 4.

46   Sequence of Events/Reading Comprehension/Animal Behaviour

Be a Detective

Look at the story on page 46.
Answer the questions.

1. A fox has four toes on each paw.
   Is the visitor a fox?   Yes   No

2. A deer has hooves.
   Is it a deer?   Yes   No

3. A raccoon has five toes on each paw.
   Is it a raccoon?   Yes   No

4. **What** did you see?

   _____

   -

   _____

5. **Where** did they come from?

   _____

   -

   _____

6. **When** did this happen?

   _____

   -

   _____

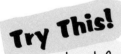

Look for tracks in your yard.
1. Go outside. Spread some sand on the ground.
2. Place bird seed, nuts, bread and fruit slices in the centre.
3. Stay away for a day. Then check for animal tracks.
4. What do you see? Three toes might mean a bird was there.

Details/Animal Characteristics

Making Cents

Count the money. Write the amounts on the lines.
Is there enough money to buy the item?
Circle **Yes** or **No**. The first one is done for you.

1. 20¢ 10¢ 10¢ 5¢   Yes (No)

2. _____ _____ _____ _____ _____   Yes   No

3. _____ _____ _____ _____ _____   Yes   No

4. _____ _____ _____ _____ _____   Yes   No

Try This!

Play Yard Sale with some friends. Use self-stick notes to label prices on things around the house. Buy and sell the things you labelled using coins or play money.

Coin Values/Addition

Write the price of each item. Then add and write the total.

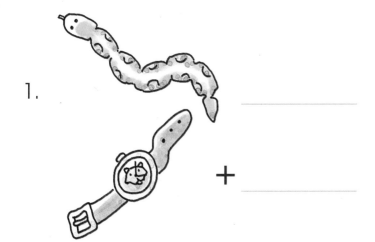

1. _____

    + _____

How much for both? _____

2. _____

    + _____

How much for both? _____

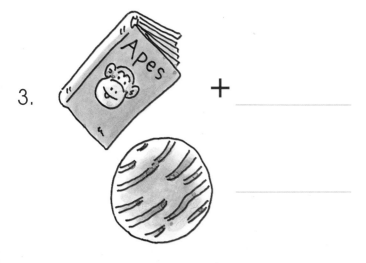

3. _____ + _____

How much for both? _____

4. _____ + _____

How much for both? _____

49

Parts of a Whole

A fraction is a part of a whole.

$\dfrac{1}{4}$ — part shaded
— parts in all

Colour the shapes to show the fractions.

$\dfrac{1}{2}$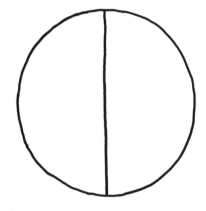

$\dfrac{1}{4}$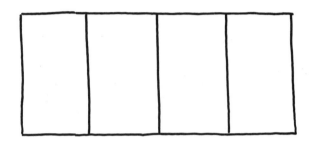

$\dfrac{1}{3}$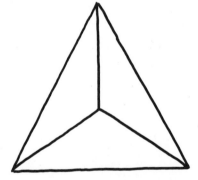

$\dfrac{2}{2}$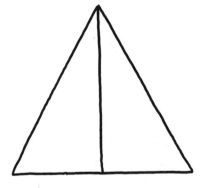

$\dfrac{3}{4}$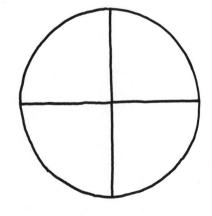

$\dfrac{2}{3}$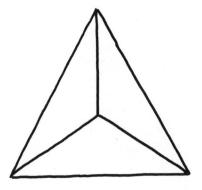

50

Fractions

Let's Eat!

What do zoo animals eat? Draw a line from each word to the food.
Colour foods in each group to show the fraction.

apples   carrots   bananas   oranges   hay   lettuce

1. $\dfrac{2}{4}$

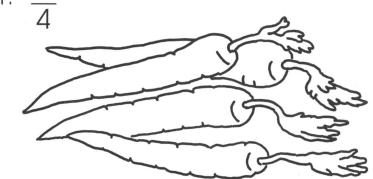

2. $\dfrac{2}{5}$

3. $\dfrac{1}{3}$

4. $\dfrac{1}{4}$

5. $\dfrac{2}{3}$

6. $\dfrac{1}{2}$

Fractions/Science Vocabulary

Butterfly Garden

Take the family through the butterfly garden. Answer each problem in the space that follows it. Then circle the hidden butterflies.

Start

8
$+4$
___

12
$-$
___
9

$4, 6, \_\_, 10$

6
-6
___

7
$+5$
___

$\frac{1}{2}$ or $\frac{1}{3}$?

Finish

How many butterflies did you find? _____

Try This!

The right half of a butterfly is the same as the left half. You need paper, scissors and crayons. Fold a sheet of paper in half. Draw half of a butterfly. Cut out the shape. Then unfold it. Colour both halves the same way.

Addition and Subtraction Review

Animal Pen Pal

Pretend you are an animal at a zoo.
Write a letter to the visitors.
Remember to sign your name as the animal.

Month   Day   Year

Date

Dear Visitors, Greeting

Body

Closing ——► Your zoo friend,

Signature ——►

A Tale of a Tail

A bear's tail is short and stubby.
One Native American tale explains why.

Once, bears  had **long, furry tails**. Then something

happened. Bear  was hungry for crayfish  .

But the pond  was frozen. So Bear  asked

Fox  for help. Tricky Fox told Bear

to make a hole in the ice. He told Bear  to hang his long

tail through the hole. When a crayfish  pinched it, he

could pull the crayfish  up. Bear  felt a

pinch. But it it was not a crayfish  . His tail was frozen into

the pond  . Bear pulled so hard that his tail

broke off. Bears  have had **short tails** ever since.

Try This!

Write your own tale. Think of an animal and what
is special about it. Tell how it got to be that way.
Draw pictures to go with your story.

Reading for Details and Cause & Effect Relationships

1. What kind of tails did bears once have?

2. What kind of tails do bears have now?

3. Why did bears' tails change?

Compare the Bears!

Black Bears: 1.2-1.5 metres long, 68-182 kilograms
Grizzly Bears: 1.8-2.2 metres long, 136-408 kilograms
Polar Bears: 1.8-2.4 metres long, up to 680 kilograms
Coastal Brown Bears: 1.8-2.6 metres long, up to 726 kilograms

Grizzly Bear

Brown Bear

Black Bear

Polar Bear

Reading for Details and Cause & Effect Relationships

Animal Count

In this picture are some of the animals
you met in this book.
Guess how many there are.

Now count the animals.
Watch out!
Some animals are hiding.
How close was your guess?

56

Be a Poet

There are many reasons people like zoos.
Write some of your reasons here to finish this poem.

Zoos

I like zoos.

I'll tell you why.

Because, _____

_____

Because, _____

_____

Because, _____

_____

Because! That's why!

I like zoos.

Try This!

Make an animal puppet to help you say your poem.
You need a paper bag, construction paper, scissors,
glue, crayons and markers. Draw a face on the flap
at the bottom of the bag.
1. Cut out and add ears.
2. Add a mouth and feet, paws or wings.
3. Put your hand inside the bag. Move the flap up and
   down to make your puppet talk.

Activities to Share: Language

Here is a list of excellent animal books to look for in your local library or bookstore. The list includes fiction and nonfiction.

- *Crocodile Smile* by Sara Weeks, illustrated by Lois Ehlert. HarperCollins, 1994. Bright picture collages enhance this book of animal songs and poems. The book comes with a cassette tape.

- *From Head to Toe* by Eric Carle. HarperCollins, 1997. A variety of familiar animals invites the reader to copy their antics as they wiggle, stomp, thump and bend across the pages of this book.

- *The Great Kapok Tree: A Tale of the Amazon Rain Forest* by Lynne Cherry. Gulliver Books, Harcourt, 1990. The great kapok tree is in danger of being cut down. What will happen to all the forest creatures if this occurs?

- *A Hippopotamusn't and Other Animal Poems* by J. Patrick Lewis. Dial Books, 1990. This is a collection of funny verse about all kinds of animals. The humorous illustrations add to the fun.

- *How the Guinea Fowl Got Her Spots: An African Tale* retold and illustrated by Barbara Knutson. Carolrhoda, 1990. When Guinea Fowl helps her friend escape from a lion, she is rewarded with a disguise that will camouflage her.

- *In the Small, Small Pond* by Denise Fleming. Henry Holt, 1993. Spring has sprung, and a bright green frog leaps out of the grass and into the pond where a host of other animals make their homes. The reader follows tadpoles, minnows, turtles, dragonflies and ducks through spring, summer and autumn. When winter arrives, the frog burrows deep into the pond to wait for spring's return.

- *Penguin Pete and Little Tim* by Marcus Pfister. North-South Books, 1994. Penguin Pete is a proud father who cannot wait to show his son the wonders of their chilly world.

- *Time to Sleep* by Denise Fleming. Henry Holt, 1997. The chill in the air tells Bear that it's time for her winter-long nap. She must tell Snail, who tells Skunk, who tells Turtle. Each puts off going to sleep in order to see, smell, hear and taste the signs of the season.

Activities to Share

🍃 *V for Vanishing: An Alphabet of Endangered Animals* by Patricia Mullins. HarperCollins, 1994. Beautiful collages depict many animals that are in danger of extinction.

Here are two videos about animals.

🍃 *The Animal Show Starring Stinky and Jake*. Polygram Home Video. Muppets Jake and Stinky host a talk show with wild animal guests.

🍃 *Really Wild Animals: Swingin' Safari*. National Geographic Kids. A globe named Spin is the host on a journey to Africa. You will see how zebras, elephants, lions and other animals grow, play and hunt for food and learn about the climatic conditions of Africa. Others in the series: *Totally Tropical Rain Forest* and *Wonders Down Under*.

Social Studies

There are many things your family can do to help preserve the environment and help save endangered animals. Here are some suggestions.

🍃 In Your Home
Recycle everything you can: newspapers, glass, cans, aluminium, motor oil, scrap metal.
Save kitchen scraps for a compost pile.
Use phosphate-free dish and laundry soaps.
Avoid using pesticides.
Use cold water in the washer whenever possible.
Use cloth napkins and washable rags.
Reuse brown paper and plastic bags.
Use plastic storage food containers rather than foil or plastic wrap.
Turn down the heat one degree for each hour you are away from home or asleep.
Turn off lights and the television when you are not in the room.
Feed the birds; make birdhouses and bird baths.
Compost leaves and yard debris.

🍃 When Shopping
Don't buy foods in plastic containers if there is an alternative.
Avoid disposable items. If you must buy disposables, buy paper rather than plastics.
Put parcels in one large sack rather than many small bags.
Buy in bulk and buy locally grown products.

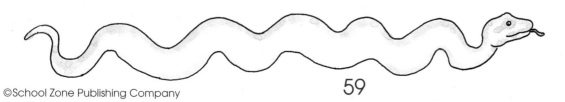

Activities to Share

Science

Some experts claim that there has been a 50% reduction in the population of song-birds over the past century. Do some simple projects with your child to house and feed some feathered friends. The world's easiest birdhouse to make uses a 15 to 20 centimetre green and orange gourd. Drill or whittle an opening for the bird. Scrape out the seeds. Drill or whittle a one centimetre drain hole at the bottom and a half centimetre hole through the top to insert a line for hanging. This house will last for one season.

To feed the birds, sew a garland of popcorn, grain cereals and dried fruits to hang in trees. Or smear peanut butter on pine cones and sprinkle with seeds.

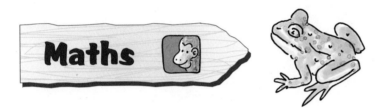

Maths

Take maths into the kitchen where you and your child can make animal-theme foods for a snack or meal. Here are two suggestions.

Hippo-Hip Hooray Salad

For each salad: 1 lettuce leaf, 1 pear half, cheese triangles, 2 raisins, 2 cherries

1. Place a lettuce leaf on a plate.
2. Top with a pear half, placing the sliced side down.
3. Add cheese triangle ears, raisin eyes and cherry nose.
   Make one salad for each family member.

A Hoot of a Treat

For each treat: 1 slice of wheat bread, tuna or chicken salad,
2 slices of egg and black olives, 1 triangle of cheese, pine nuts

1. Cut the bread on one end to form owl's head.
2. Cover the bread with a favourite spread.
3. Place 2 egg slices with black olive slices for eyes.
4. Add a cheese beak and pine nuts for claws. Enjoy!

Activities to Share

Contents

Language

Social Studies

Maths

Science

And More

Summer Fun

Dani and Josh live on Shady Lane.
Three friends live there, too.

School is out! Summer fun begins!
Circle the friends' names in the puzzle.

```
S  T  W  E  N  W
B  I  L  L  Y  T
L  P  E  D  R  O
K  C  D  A  N  I
G  J  O  S  H  J
```

HOT IDEA

Make a word puzzle using the names of friends. Ask one friend to solve the puzzle.

Draw a picture of your favourite summertime activity.

Follow the Friends

What does each friend like to do in the summer?
Write a letter from the box to finish each word.

b h s c f r

_____ wim

_____

_____ amp

_____ ish

_____

_____ ide

_____ ike

_____

_____ aseball

What do you like to do?

_____

_____

HOT idea

Think of things you can do with a group of friends. Try to put on a magic show, go star gazing, plant a garden or have a garage sale.

Here Comes Summer!

What things go with summer?
Draw a line from each picture to the sun.

beach
towel

baseball cap

mittens

shorts

boots

suitcase

watermelon

beach ball

picnic

HOT
IDEA

Write a summer poem:
Bright hot sun.
Campers having fun.
Swimmers on the go.
NO cold snow!

snowman

swimsuit

64

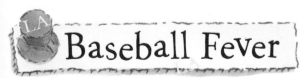

It is time for baseball practice. Dani and Josh run outside.
Read the sentences. Write each friend's name by his or her house.

Dani and Josh

Billy has a flower garden. 🌸🌸   His house is blue. 🟦

Pedro has a pond. 🐸   His house is red. 🟥

Wen has a fence. 🏳   Her house is yellow. ⬜

GiGGLES

Josh: Mum, may I go out and play?
Mum: With those holes in your socks?
Josh: No, with Billy, Pedro and Wen!
For more riddles, doodles & guessing game fun, visit the website:
www.droodles.com

Sentence Comprehension

Go Team!

The five friends play for the Rockets.
Write the team number on each child's
team shirt.

Dani is number **six**.
Josh is number **one**.
Pedro is number **three**.
Billy is number **eight**.
Wen is number **seven**.

There are **9** players on a baseball team.
How many more players are needed to play a game? _____

COOL FACT

The Baseball Hall of Fame
is in Cooperstown, New York.

Buffalo
Syracuse
Cooperstown
New York City

Number Recognition

Batter Up!

Read what each friend says.
Write their names in order.

I bat third.

I bat first!

I bat after Dani.

I bat fourth.

I bat before Wen.

Batting Order

1. _____

2. _____

3. _____

4. _____

5. _____

GiGGLES

How is a baseball game like a pancake?

They both need the batter.

Ordinal Numbers

Keeping Score

The Rockets played their first game with the Flyers.
Add to fill in the missing numbers.

INNING	Rockets	Flyers	TOTAL RUNS
1	1		3
2		2	4
3	1		1
4		0	2
5		3	5
6	1		2
7			
8			
9			
TOTAL			17

How many innings did they play? _____
_____

Who won the game? _____

After the game, the Rockets were hungry.
Circle the coins needed to buy each item.
Use the fewest coins you can.

Five-cent coin = 5¢   Ten-cent coin = 10¢   Twenty-cent coin = 20¢   Dollar coin = $1.00

1.

2.

3.

4.

69   Counting Money

Splash City

The water park opens today!
From 1–6, number the names in ABC order.

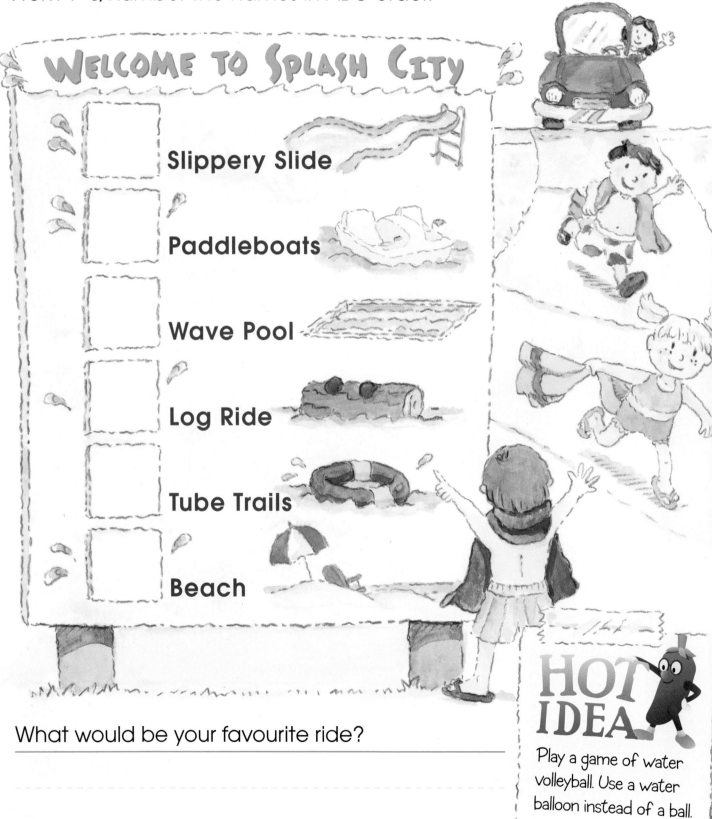

WELCOME TO SPLASH CITY

- [ ] **Slippery Slide**
- [ ] **Paddleboats**
- [ ] **Wave Pool**
- [ ] **Log Ride**
- [ ] **Tube Trails**
- [ ] **Beach**

What would be your favourite ride?

_____

_____

HOT IDEA

Play a game of water volleyball. Use a water balloon instead of a ball.

ABC Order

Slippery Slide Ride

Help Wen get down the water slide.
Circle word pairs that rhyme.
Then draw a line to connect the word pairs.

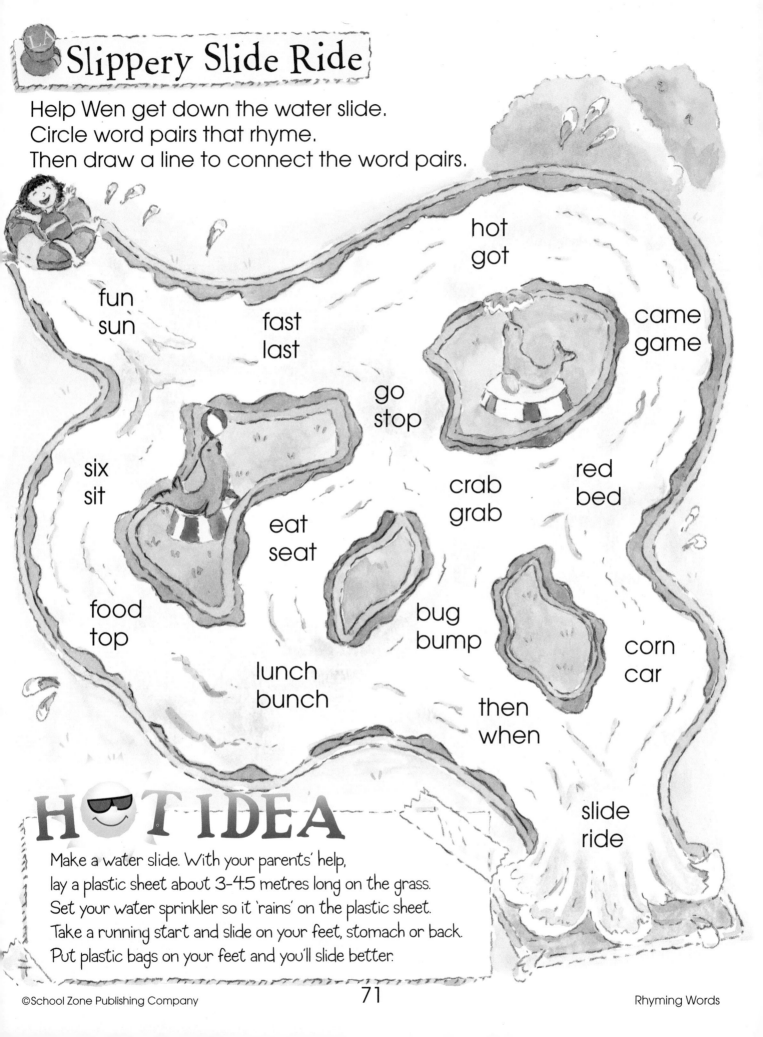

hot
got

fun
sun

fast
last

came
game

six
sit

go
stop

red
bed

crab
grab

eat
seat

food
top

bug
bump

corn
car

lunch
bunch

then
when

slide
ride

HOT IDEA

Make a water slide. With your parents' help,
lay a plastic sheet about 3-4.5 metres long on the grass.
Set your water sprinkler so it 'rains' on the plastic sheet.
Take a running start and slide on your feet, stomach or back.
Put plastic bags on your feet and you'll slide better.

Rhyming Words

Ride the Waves

Read each word in the wave pool.

loud

in

fast

happy

cool

big

Write a word from the pool that means the opposite.

1. out _____

2. warm _____

3. little _____

4. quiet _____

5. slow _____

HOT IDEA

Play baseball in your yard. In place of a ball use a water balloon.

6. sad _____

Draw yourself in the wave pool with a friend.

72

Antonyms

That's Not Right!

Look at the wave pool. What's not right?
Circle up to 8 things that don't look right.

No Running

Write one pool rule.

_____

_____

_____

H☻T IDEA

You don't want to get too much sun on a hot summer day. Make a sun hat for yourself.
You will need a piece of newspaper (two pages with a fold down the middle).

1. Fold the outer edge down to make a point at the top centre.

2. Fold the bottom flap up to meet the bottom of the triangle.

3. Then fold it over again.

4. Do the same on the other side.

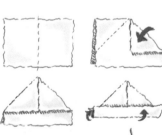

Safety Awareness

Off to the Dude Ranch

Pedro and his family are spending a week at Circle S Ranch. Answer the questions to help them get to the riding stables.

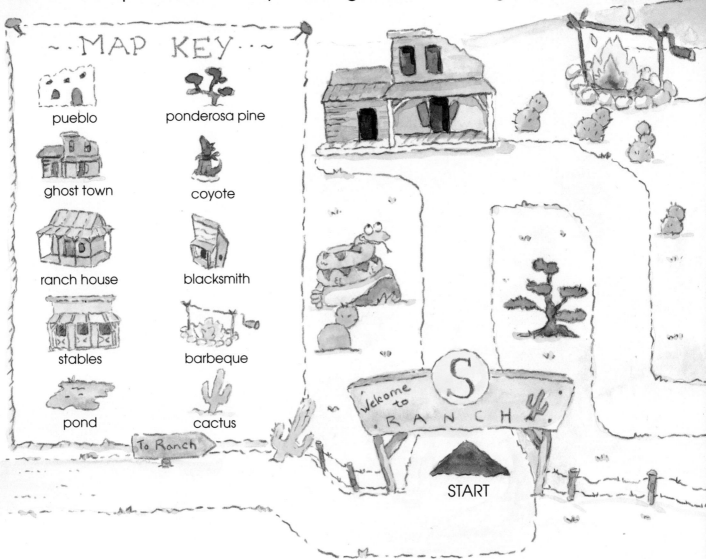

1. What will they pass first?   ghost town   cows

2. Will they turn at the ranch house?   yes   no

3. Will they cross over a bridge?   yes   no

4. What will they pass after the bridge?   coyote   pueblo

5. What is the last thing they will pass?   barbeque pit   pond

Draw a line to show the path.

Map Skills/Comprehension

What two things would you
like to see at Circle S Ranch?

_____

_____

_____

COOL FACT

There are more than 130
ghost towns in the US state
New Mexico!

Map Skills/Comprehension

Giddyup!

Draw a line between two horses that make a compound word.

sun

top

after

down

down

hill

noon

tree

HOT IDEA

Whether you are riding or walking the trail, make a nutty mix to take along for a snack. Chop up favourite chocolate or museli bars. Add mixed nuts, bite-size crackers, dried fruits and cereal. YUM!

76

Saving for Souvenirs

Josh and Dani saved money for a family trip.
Count the money each one has.
Write the amounts on the lines.

One dollar coins

$ _____

One dollar coins

$ _____

Twenty-cent coins

_____ ¢

Twenty-cent coins

_____ ¢

Ten-cent coins

_____ ¢

Ten-cent coins

_____ ¢

Five-cent coins

_____ ¢

Five-cent coins

_____ ¢

Josh's Total: $ _____

Dani's Total: $ _____

HOT IDEA

To make a great souvenir of your summer travels, take along a cap and a permanent marker. Ask new friends you meet along the way to sign your cap.

Who saved more?

_____

_____

_____

Camping Out!

Dani and Josh went on a family camping trip.
Use the map to answer the questions.

1. A camper is by the playground.   yes   no

2. There is a path to the lake.   yes   no

3. The hiking trail is near the camp store.   yes   no

Reading Maps

4. Tents and campers are in the same area.   yes   no

5. The picnic area is near the tree fort.   yes   no

6. A bath house is by the lake.   yes   no

Reading Maps

Summer at the Seashore

Wen's family took a trip to the beach.
Name the beach things Wen sees.
Colour the pictures to finish the patterns.

Draw and colour the pictures to finish the patterns.

_____

_____

GiGGLES

Knock, knock!
Who's there?
Shell.
Shell who?
She'll be coming round the
mountain when she comes!

_____

80

Patterns

On the Beach

Wen and her family saw many things at the beach. Write the name of each thing on the chart.

OKAY FOR SWIMMING

flag

kite

boat

lifeguard

seagulls

crab

shells

COOL FACT

Hermit crabs don't make their own shells. They find a shell that fits and move in. If they don't, they might be eaten by a gull!

Living things	Non-living things

Dig In!

Wen and her brother like to build sandcastles.
Write the numerals 1–5 to tell the order in which things happen.

Sequencing

As a Matter of Fact

Read each animal fact. Use the vowel code to write the animal name. Write the sentence number in the box next to the animal it describes.

a	e	i	o	u
●	▲	★	◆	■

1. I have eight arms and large eyes.

   ◆ c t ◆ p ■ s _____

2. I blow myself up when I am scared.

   b l ◆ w f ★ s h _____

3. I have a soft body, so I find a shell to live in.

   h ▲ r m ★ t c r ● b _____

4. I have sharp teeth on my snout.

   s ● w f ★ s h _____

5. I talk with whistles, chirps and other sounds.

   d ◆ l p h ★ n _____

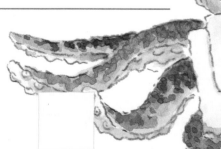

COOL FACT

Starfish do not have a brain.

Sea Animals/Vowels

Travel Tips

Billy's family is planning a trip. They read about different places. Write the missing word from the box.

Island   **Mountain**   Desert   Forest

In Coyote

_____

_____

Camping Is Great

In **Black Bear**

_____

_____

Turtle

_____

_____

A great place to visit!

Climb

GIANT

_____

_____

Landform Recognition

Different Places

Fill in the missing word to complete each sentence.
Use the words in the box to help you.

water   dry
cold   hot
trees

1. It's very _____ high in the mountains.

2. Deserts are _____ during the day.

3. The sand is _____ from lack of rain.

4. Islands are surrounded by _____.

5. Forests are lands with _____.

GiGGLES

How is an island
like the letter t?

Both are in the middle
of water.

Where does Billy's family go?
Unscramble the letters and write the words: **t o y o e C e s D r t e**

Landform Recognition

Getting There

Summer is a good time to travel. People go from place to place across the country. What different kinds of transportation do they use?

Read each rhyme. Then write the name of the transportation it describes.

1. I rhyme with hike. _____

2. I rhyme with us. _____

3. I rhyme with star. _____

4. I rhyme with pet. _____

5. I rhyme with plane. _____

Transportation/Rhyming Words

Travel Shapes

Follow the directions to draw a jet and a ship.

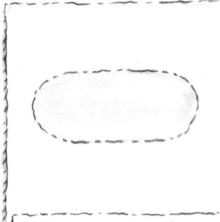

1. Draw an oval.

2. Add five triangles.

3. Draw squares for windows. Add some clouds.

Where would you like a jet to take you?

_____

1. Draw five rectangles.

2. Add two triangles.

3. Draw ten circles. Add some waves.

Where would you like a ship to take you?

_____

_____

Wish You Were Here!

Read each postcard. Draw a line to match the card with the friend who wrote it. Write the friend's name on the card.

Howdy,
    This ranch is lots of fun. I ride a horse named Sugarlump. I learned to rope a calf. Tonight there is a cookout.

_____

_____

Hi,
    We are having a great time camping. We saw deer and a bear yesterday. Wish you were here.

_____

_____

_____

_____

WEN'S CASTLE

Write words from the box to answer the questions.

ocean	calf	bear	horse	desert

_____

_____

1. Dani and Josh saw what animal? _____

_____

2. Where did Wen swim? _____

Reading Comprehension

Hi,
    The desert is fantastic. One cactus is taller than my house! I heard a coyote last night. See you soon.

_____

- -

_____

Hi,
    The ocean is great! I swim every day. I have made three sandcastles. Wish you were here to look for seashells.

_____

- -

_____

SUGARLUMP

HOT IDEA

If you could build a bridge from your house to anywhere in the world, where would it be? Why?

_____

3. What animal did Pedro rope? _____

_____

4. Who is Sugarlump? _____

_____

5. Where does a cactus grow? _____

Gone Fishing

The five friends were home from their trips. They went fishing. Read the picture graph. Write the number of fish each one caught.

Children	🐟 = 2 fish	Number of Fish

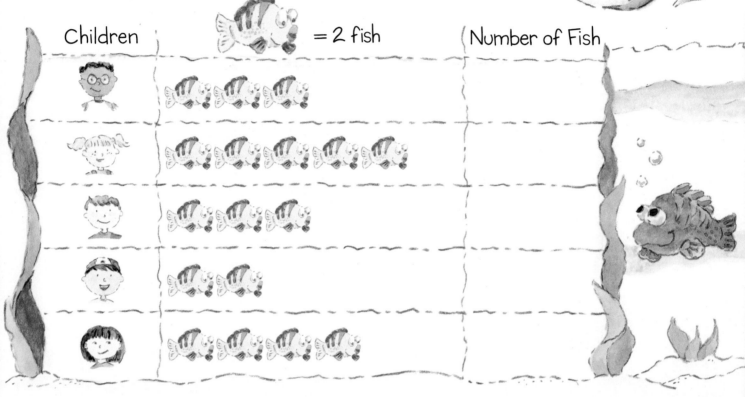

1. Who caught the most fish?

2. Who caught the fewest fish?

3. Who caught the same number of fish?

GiGGLES

What's the difference between a piano and a fish?

You can tune a piano, but you can't tuna fish!

Picture Graphs/Counting by Twos

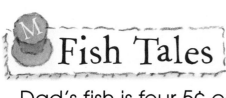
Fish Tales

Dad's fish is four 5¢ coins long.

Estimate how many 5¢ coins long each fish is.
Now measure with 5¢ coins.
How close was your guess?

Estimate	Measure

COOL FACT

When a fish called a flounder hatches, it has one eye on each side of its head. After living on the bottom of the sea, one eye twists around so that both eyes are on one side of the flounder's head.

Estimation

Nature Spy

Josh and Wen are looking for insects.
Not all bugs are insects.

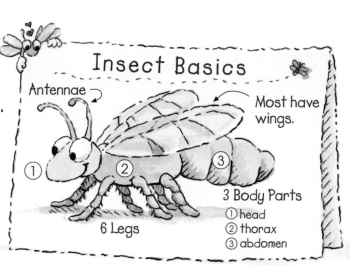

Insect Basics

Antennae

Most have wings.

① ② ③

6 Legs

3 Body Parts
① head
② thorax
③ abdomen

Check the boxes next to the bugs
that are insects.

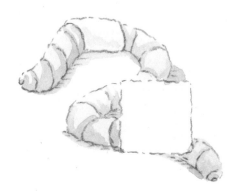

COOL FACT

A click beetle has a special talent.
If it is on its back, it will slowly bend
in the middle and pop straight up into
the air with a loud 'click!'

Insect Identification

Buggy Backyard

Josh and Wen decided to be detectives for the day.
Look at the picture. Circle the hidden insects.

How many insects did you find?

Go outside. Look at an insect with a magnifying glass.
Draw what you see.

COOL FACT

The firebrat really is a brat if it gets into your
home. It likes to eat wallpaper paste, crackers and
clothes! The whirligig beetle twirls around in a pond
making zigzag patterns.

Rub-a-Dub-Dub

Josh and Dani planned a neighbourhood dog wash.
Read the sentences. Draw a line to show where they go.

1. First, they go to Mrs Green's.
2. Next, they go to Mr Berry's.
3. Then, they go to the Ride house.
4. Last, they go to Mrs Ball's.

Rub-a-dub-dub,
Washing dogs in a tub.
Rub-a-dub-dub,
How many dogs did they scrub? _____ dogs

Following Directions/Sequence

This calendar tells what is happening where the friends live.

Sunday	Monday	Tuesday	Wednesday	Thursday	Friday	Saturday
Berry picking at Eno Farm	Farmers' Market opens today!	Berry Baking Contest	Parade 11:00	Fireworks at the lake 9:00	Fair starts today	Blue Ribbon Day at the Fair

Write the day when these things happen.

1.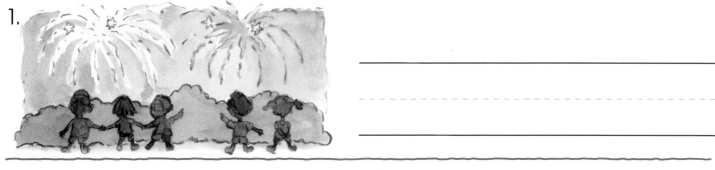

_____

- - - - - - - - - - - - - - - - - -

_____

2.

_____

- - - - - - - - - - - - - - - - - -

_____

3.

_____

- - - - - - - - - - - - - - - - - -

_____

4.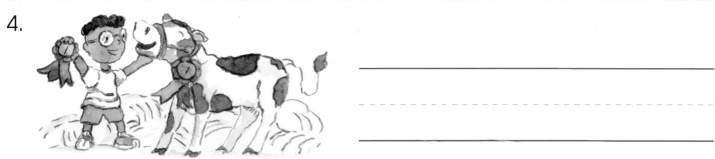

_____

- - - - - - - - - - - - - - - - - -

_____

Weather

This is a picture graph about the weather in November.

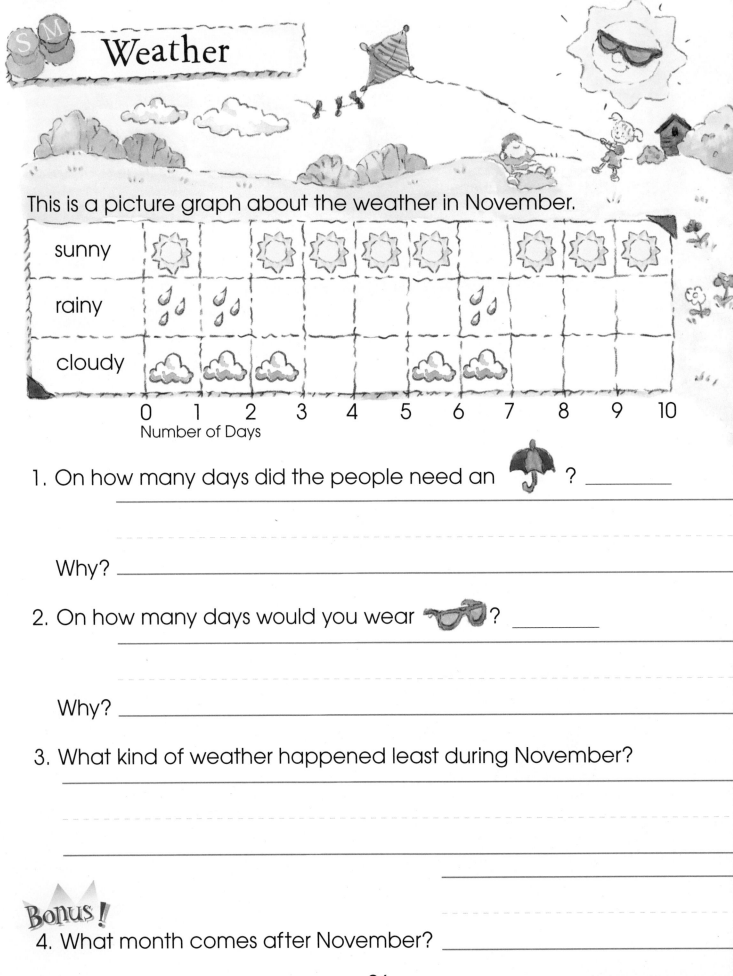

Number of Days

1. On how many days did the people need an ☂? _____

   _____

   Why? _____

2. On how many days would you wear 👓? _____

   _____

   Why? _____

3. What kind of weather happened least during November?

   _____

   _____

   _____

Bonus!

4. What month comes after November? _____

Interpreting a Picture Graph

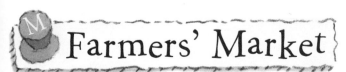

Farmers' Market

Write each sum. Colour the picture.

1. 8 + 3 = _____

2. 11 − 3 = _____

3. 6 + 6 = _____

4. 12 − 6 = _____

5. 5 + 4 = _____

6. 9 − 4 = _____

HOT IDEA

Make maths flashcards you can solve and eat! Spread peanut butter on digestive biscuits. Use licorice whips to form a number problem. Solve the problem and eat!

Sums and Differences

One Potato, Two Potatoes

Write the food names in ABC order.
Write the numeral to tell how many.

potatoes

carrots

apples

melons

lettuce

bananas

Food in ABC order	How many?

HOT IDEA

Count the numbers of fruits and vegetables again. This time count backwards! 3-2-1 melons!

Counting/ABC Order

Graph It!

Fill in the graph. Colour one box for each fruit and vegetable on page 98.

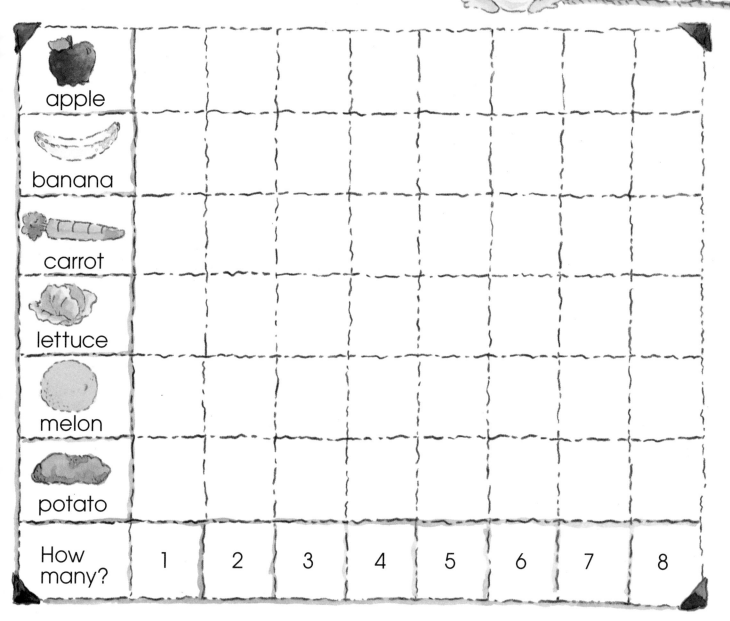

	1	2	3	4	5	6	7	8
apple								
banana								
carrot								
lettuce								
melon								
potato								
How many?	1	2	3	4	5	6	7	8

Circle the correct answer.

1. Are there more apples or potatoes?

2. Are there more melons or heads of lettuce?

3. Are there fewer carrots or bananas?

4. Are there fewer apples or carrots?

Graphing/More Than and Less Than

How Many?

The friends saw many kinds of fruits and vegetables.
Write how many of each.

1. _____ tens _____ ones

How many? _____

2. _____ tens _____ ones

How many? _____

3. _____ tens _____ ones

How many? _____

4. _____ tens _____ ones

How many? _____

5. _____ tens _____ ones

How many? _____

6. _____ tens _____ ones

How many? _____

How many tens? How many ones?

	tens	ones
40		
36		

Place Value

Bunches of Berries

Billy and Pedro went berry picking.
Pedro made piles of 5 berries. Count by fives.
Write the numbers.

5

How many did Pedro pick?_____

Billy made piles of 10 berries. Count by tens.
Write the numbers.

10

How many did Billy pick?_____

HOT IDEA

Juicy Painting
Mash blueberries through a sieve. Use the juice to
paint a picture. What colour is the juice?

Berry Good Muffins

Billy and Pedro made blueberry muffins for their friends.
Read what they did. Number the steps 1–4.

Bake until golden brown.

First, mix the batter.

Next, add the blueberries.

Then, pour into muffin cups.

HOT IDEA

Make Your Own Blueberry Muffins   *Parent-Supervised Activity!

You need:

1 3/4 cups flour	1/2 tsp salt	2 eggs
1/3 cup sugar	1/4 cup cooking oil	1 tsp vanilla
2 tsps baking powder	3/4 cup milk	1 cup blueberries

1. Heat oven to 400°F/200°C. Put 12 paper baking cups in muffin tin.
2. Combine the dry ingredients.
3. Mix the oil, milk, eggs and vanilla together.
4. Add wet mixture to dry ingredients. Stir in berries.
5. Pour into muffin cups.
6. Bake 20–25 minutes or until golden brown. YUM!

Sequence

Hooray, Hooray, for Australia Day!

Each year on 26 January we celebrate our nation.

A sentence has a **naming part**.
The naming part tells who or what the sentence is about.
Write the naming part of each sentence.

1. The parade begins at 2:00 P.M.   parade

2. Pedro will carry the flag.

3. Drums will be played.

4. Bells will ring.

5. Our town loves a parade.

103   Sentence/Naming Part

Party Time!

Read the invitation.

COME TO A PARTY!

What: Australia Day picnic

When: 26 January at 2:00 P.M.

Where: 123 Shady Lane

Who: Wen Chu

Bring your favourite picnic food.

Circle the answer to each question.

1. Who is having a party?   Billy   Wen

2. What is the party for?   holiday   birthday

3. What day is the party?   26 July   26 January

4. What time is the party?   2:00 P.M.   12:00 P.M.

5. Where will the party be?   123 Shady Lane   Billy's house

What picnic food will you bring to the party?

_____

_____

_____

GiGGLES

Where can a burger get a great night's sleep?

On a bed of lettuce

Backyard Barbeque

A sentence has a **telling part**.
The telling part tells what someone or something does.

Underline the telling part of each sentence.

1. Dani <u>brings milk</u>.

2. Josh has bananas.

3. Wen takes a salad.

4. Billy carries hot dogs.

5. They all eat together.

Write a sentence about a picnic.
Underline the telling part.

_____

_____

_____

Bonus!

Who didn't bring anything?_____

Sentence/Telling Part

Ka-Boom!

What are the friends saying about the fireworks?
Use words from the box to write each contraction.

Isn't   **Don't**   **We're**   **Let's**   **I'm**

_____
- - - - - - - - - - - - - - -
_____ watch!
Let us

_____
- - - - - - - - - - - - - - -
_____ this great?
Is not

_____
- - - - - - - - - - - - - - -
_____ blink!
Do not

_____
- - - - - - - - - - - - - - -
_____ lucky!
We are

_____
- - - - - - - - - - - - - - -
_____ watching!
I am

HOT IDEA

Make a Spinner
You need string, scissors, crepe paper and a spring clothes-pin.
1. Cut a piece of string as long as your arm.
2. Thread the string through the hole in the clothes-pin and tie a knot.
3. Cut crepe paper strips as tall as you.
4. Clip the clothes-pin to one end of the strips.
5. Hold the end of the string and wave your arm to twirl the strips.

106

Contractions

Write the time next to each clock.
Draw a line to match the clock to what happens.

1. _____ o'clock

2. _____ o'clock

3. _____ o'clock

4. _____ o'clock

5. _____ o'clock

PIE JUDGING 10:00

ROPING CONTEST 11:00

TRACTOR PULL 2:00

MAGIC SHOW 5:00

BANDSTAND 6:00

GiGGLES

What do you tell a clock at noon?

Hands up!

Telling Time: Hour

County Fair!

What is the most popular event at the fair?
Colour one box for each person.

Graphing

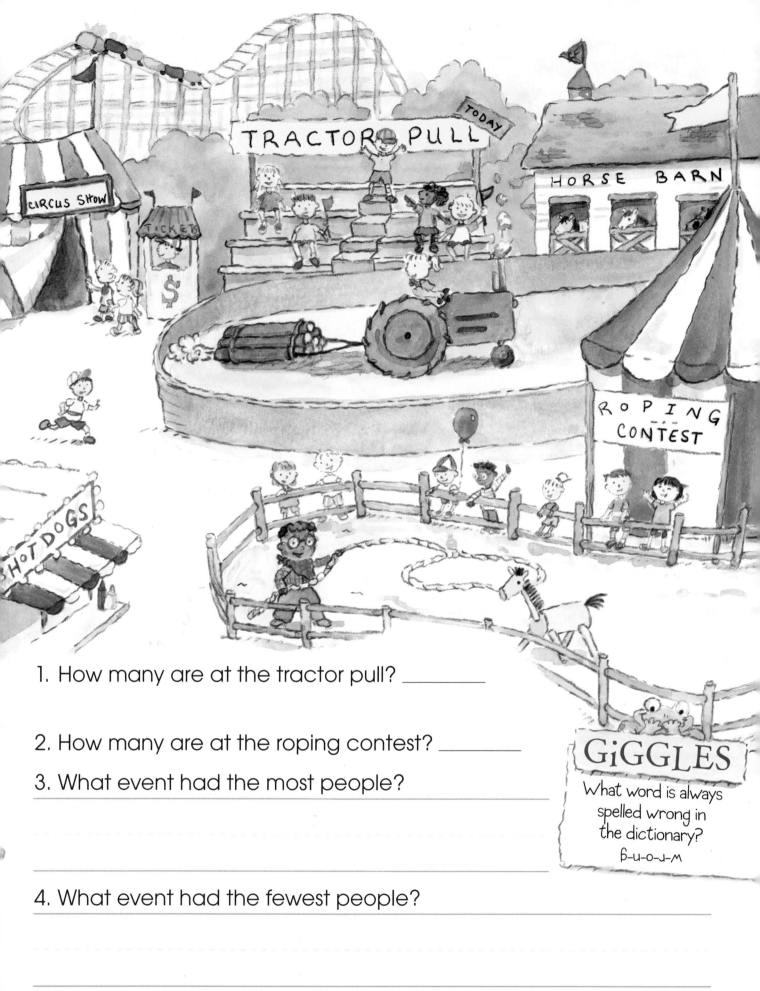

1. How many are at the tractor pull? _____

2. How many are at the roping contest? _____

3. What event had the most people? _____

_____

4. What event had the fewest people? _____

_____

GiGGLES

What word is always spelled wrong in the dictionary?

w-r-o-n-g

Interpreting Graphs

What a Ride!

Write the time.

1. half past _____

_____ : _____

2. half past _____

_____ : _____

3. half past _____

_____ : _____

Draw hands to show the time.

4. 8:00

5. 11:30

6. 3:00

7. 4:30

GiGGLES

What goes up but never comes down?

Your age!

How Much?

Fill in the number of coins Billy needs to have the correct amount.

Clyde's Carnival Treasures

	$1.00 coin	20¢ coin	10¢ coin	5¢ coin
10¢	0	0	1	0
15¢				
35¢				
40¢				
$1.75				
$2.50				

H☀T IDEA

Set up a pretend auction with your friends. Collect items that will go up for bid. You be the first auctioneer and have your friends make bids on an object. The highest bidder counts out the correct amount of play money to pay. The highest bidder then becomes auctioneer and the bidding begins on a new item.

Counting Money

Animals at the Fair

Write the naming word for the animals at the fair. Use the words in the box if you need to.

pig   horse
dog   duck
cow   goat

_____

1. The _____ is tall.
_____

2. A _____ is fat!
_____

3. The _____ has horns.
_____

4. A spotted _____ moos.
_____

5. The _____ eats corn.
_____

6. Is the _____ lost?

Sentence/Naming Part

My, My, What a Pie!

Circle the correct pizza.

1. Billy and Pedro get an equal share.
   How did they cut the pizza?

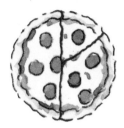         

2. Dani, Josh and Wen get an equal share.
   How did they cut the pizza?

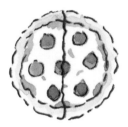   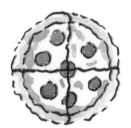      

3. Billy, Dani, Wen and Josh get an equal share.
   How did they cut the pizza?

   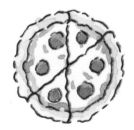      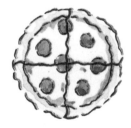

4. Circle the picture that shows $\frac{2}{3}$ of the apples coloured.

Fractions

Growing, Growing...

Josh grew a watermelon. In the spring, he planted seeds. He watered his plant each day. The sun made it grow. By summer, the watermelon was huge! He brought it to the fair. He won a blue ribbon!

Circle the answer.

1. Who is the story about?

   a. Dani   b. Josh   c. Pedro

2. What fruit was grown?

   a. apples   b. watermelon   c. bananas

3. What did the plant need?

   a. water, rain, clouds   b. soil, sun, plants   c. soil, water, sun

4. Write 1, 2, 3, 4 to show the order.

COOL FACT

The saguaro cactus can grow more than 18 metres tall!

Plants/Main Ideas

Crafty Winners

Look at the front of each birdhouse.
Write how many sides, corners and
square corners you can see for each.

1.

_____ sides

_____ corners

_____ square corners

2.

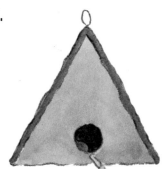

_____ sides

_____ corners

_____ square corners

3.

_____ sides

_____ corners

_____ square corners

4.

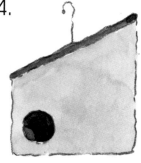

_____ sides

_____ corners

_____ square corners

5.

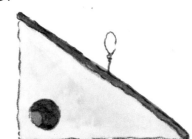

_____ sides

_____ corners

_____ square corners

6.

_____ sides

_____ corners

_____ square corners

GiGGLES

When you do not eat much, it is said you
eat like me. But I am always eating, when
I'm not nesting in a tree. Who am I?

A bird.

Geometric Shapes

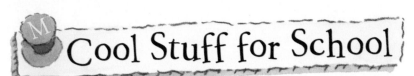

Cool Stuff for School

BACK-TO-School Supplies

Summer is over. School will start soon.
The friends are doing some back-to-school shopping.

Use the grid on page 117 to see where each thing is
found. Write the aisle and row to find each item.
The first one is done for you.

1. Find the  . Aisle __3__ Row __3__

2. Find the . Aisle _____ Row _____

3. Find the . Aisle _____ Row _____

4. Find the . Aisle _____ Row _____

5. Find the . Aisle _____ Row _____

6. Find the . Aisle _____ Row _____

7. Find the . Aisle _____ Row _____

8. Find the . Aisle _____ Row _____

Coordinates

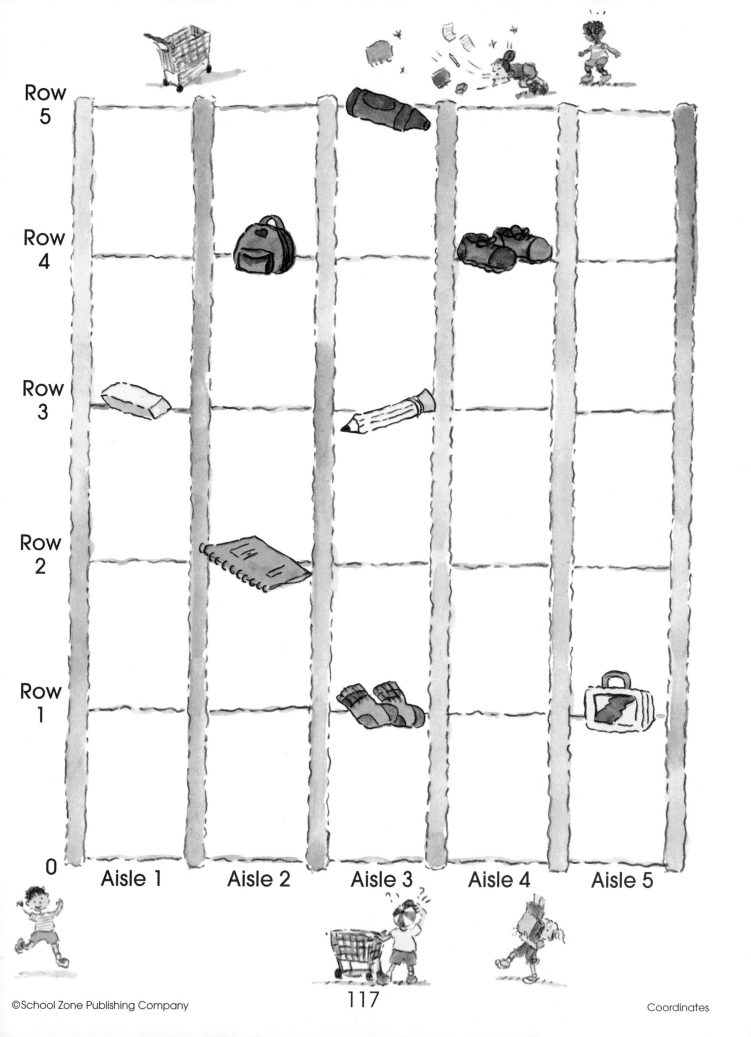

Row 5

Row 4

Row 3

Row 2

Row 1

0

Aisle 1   Aisle 2   Aisle 3   Aisle 4   Aisle 5

Coordinates

Back to School

Use <u>was</u> to tell about one.
Use <u>were</u> to tell about more than one.

Write in the correct verb to complete each sentence.

_____

1. The friends _____ ready for school.

2. Dani _____ walking to school.

3. Pedro _____ waiting for Billy.

4. Wen and Josh _____ talking on the bus.

5. They _____ all happy to be back in school.

Next Summer

Use a full stop (.) to end a sentence that tells.
Use a (?) to end a sentence that asks.
Use this mark ≡ to show where a capital letter goes.

Correct the sentences below by adding the proper marks.
The first one is done for you.

1. did you have a nice summer?
   ≡

2. name one thing you did

3. will you take a trip next summer

4. do you know where you will go

5. i hope you have lots of fun

6. Write a sentence about what you did this summer.

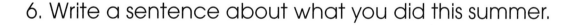

Activities to Share

Here is a list of books with a summer theme, including books about the summer season, sport and travel. The list includes fiction and nonfiction selections for you to check out at your local library or bookstore. You can also find out about cool books and a summer reading club at **www.kidsreads.com**

Summer

• *52 Fun Things to Do at a Beach* by Lynn Gordon and illustrated by Karen Johnson. Chronicle Books, 1999. There are instructions for making sand dough, casting shadow monsters, sculpting portraits and much more.

• *Crafts to Make in the Summer* by Kathy Ross and illustrated by Vicky Enright. Millbrook Press, 1999. Wonderful instructions and illustrations offer 29 easy-to-make craft projects with summertime themes, including a sunglasses case, a seashell candle holder and a firecracker finger puppet.

• *How Do You Know It's Summer?* (Rookie Read About Science) by Allan Fowler. Children's Press, 1992. Children will recognise the typical signs of summer presented in this book, such as heat, thunderstorms, playtime, growing and outdoor fun.

• *The Kids Summer Games Book* by Jane Drake and Ann Love and illustrated by Heather Collins. Kids Can Press, 1998. Your child will find hundreds of fun things to do in this book, including games to play with friends, alone, on the beach or in the water, as well as activities to do outside in the sun and indoors on rainy days.

Sport

• *Bats About Baseball* by Jean Little and Claire MacKay and illustrated by Kim Lafave. Viking, 1995. Ryder's grandmother goes nuts over baseball.

• *Playing Right Field* by Willy Welch and illustrated by Marc Simont. Scholastic, 1995. A boy daydreams about making a great play way out in right field.

Travel

When your family is on the road, you might want to check out these titles to provide your children with lots of things to do along the way!

• *52 Fun Things to Do in the Car* by Lynn Gordon and illustrated by Susan Synarski. Chronicle Books, 1994, and *52 Fun Things to Do on the Plane* by Lynn Gordon. Chronicle Books, 1996. The books deliver just as their titles suggest – lots of fun things to keep the little traveller busy!

Not just books! Check out these videos.

Videos

Casey at the Bat
(CBS/Fox/Playhouse Video)
It's 1888 and Casey Frank saves Mudville's stadium and starts traditions we still see at baseball games today.

Let's Go Camping
(Vermont Storyworks 1-800-206-8383)
Ranger Ben offers information to take a fun and safe camping trip.

Social Studies

• A Day at the Beach

Cool breezes, the smell of fresh salt air, the feel of sand between your toes – it's all at the beach! If you are planning a trip to the beach, here are a few tips for your family.

What to Bring: Make a list of things to bring, including sunscreen, sunglasses, towels, hats, pails, things to dig with, long-sleeved shirts and full-length trousers that are light and loose to wear exploring, and something to wear if the air turns cool once the sun goes down.

To make great sandcastles, contact the experts at **www.unlitter.com**

Science

• *A Kid's Summer Ecojournal: With Nature Activities for Exploring the Season* by Toni Albert. Trickle Creek Books, 1998.
This book will encourage your child to explore, read and write about nature. Activities include making a map, growing a flower, harvesting seeds, baking a potato with solar heat, collecting fireflies, following snails and more.

• *High Tide, Low Tide* by Mick Manning. The Watts Publishing Group, 2003.
If you and your family like to look for treasures on the beach, the best beachcombing happens right after the tide goes out during low tide. This is when you are likely to find treasures the high tide left behind. Look on the weather page of your local newspaper for the time of the tides.

Here are a few cool websites to check out:
For a close-up look at sea animals, visit **www.seaworld.com**
For lots of fishy fun, visit **www.tetra-fish.com**

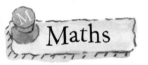

Maths

• Rainbow Snack
Measure and mix these ingredients for a tasty anytime snack.

1 cup of coloured fruit-flavoured puffed cereal

1 cup of fruit-flavoured cereal shaped like Os

1/2 cup sunflower seeds

1/2 cup peanuts or mixed nuts

1/2 cup raisins and other dried fruits

Place all the ingredients in a small plastic bag. Give it a good shake. Your snack is ready for travel!

Activities to Share

Answers

Pages 2–3
Bank, Fire Station, Grocery, Hospital, Post Office, School, Toy Shop, Zippity Zoo

Pages 4–5

4. Answers will vary.
5. yes
6. yes
7. no

Page 6
1. swan 2. bobcat 3. zebra

Page 9
number words: five, one, four, four, one, three, three, one, two, two, one, one, one

words that rhyme with tip: 1. dip
2. slip 3. trip 4. flip; other words: chip, clip, drip, hip, grip, lip, nip, rip, ship, sip, skip, snip, yip, zip

Page 7

Page 8
fast, stop, top, pat, ten, tent, tub, bat at, trap, rap, pot; *counterclockwise*: fat, top, par, part, tab, but, net, tap, pot, pots

Page 10
1. 3	2. 6
3. 3 or 8	4. 2
5. 4	6. 1

Page 13
1. under 2. on 3. over
4. across 5. in

Page 12
missing numerals: 4, 3, 6, 5, 6, 9, 6, 10, 8, 11, 6

Page 16
$4 + 3 = 7$ tigers
$6 + 3 = 9$ leopards
$4 + 2 = 6$ bobcats
$5 + 4 = 9$ lions

Page 11
1. snake 2. swan
3. spider 4. skunk
5. slug 6. starfish

```
x  b  s  k  u  n  k
v  s  t  o  p  s  g
s  w  a  n  g  n  s
f  t  r  y  c  o  l
t  u  f  z  j  w  u
s  p  i  d  e  r  g
y  o  s  n  a  k  e
p  q  h  s  n  a  p
```

Page 15
1. Jungle World
2. Quackers Pond
3. Zebra Park
4. Monkey Island
   Bear Cave

Pages 17–18
1. Names will vary.	2. $1 + 2 = 3$
3. $3 - 1 = 2$	4. $2 + 3 = 5$
5. $5 - 2 = 3$	6. $3 + 3 = 6$
7. $6 - 2 = 4$	8. $4 - 4 = 0$

Page 14
Circle Jan, Bob, Chan and Lisa.
1. Bob 2. Jan 3. Lisa 4. Chan

Page 19
1. slide
2. jump
3. dig
4. climb

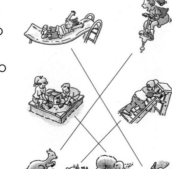

Page 20

1. pup 2. cub

Answers

Pages 21–22

1. robin
2. fish
3. snake
4. chick

Page 25

1. 6 + 4 = 10   2. 5 - 4 = 1
3. 4 + 2 = 6   4. 5 - 3 = 2
5. 7 + 5 = 12   6. 5 - 2 = 3

Page 26

1. wet   2. huge
3. tiny   4. sleepy
5. long   6. tall

Page 30

tiger cub										
baby porcupine										
fox										
snowy owl										
fawn										
opossum										
weight in kilograms	1	2	3	4	5	6	7	8	9	10

Pages 32–33

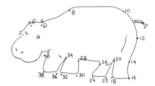

mountain; tiger; 12; river or stream; porcupine; 5; palm tree;
zebra; box or fox; 8; rainbow; anteater; bear or bare;
pond; 9; 1; trees or forest; panda; 6; snake; tulip
or flower; penguin; block or black; waterfall; sheep

Page 23

1. can't — can not
2. Let's — Let us
3. Where's — Where is
4. isn't — is not

Page 27

1. 14
2. 2

Page 31

Put in	Take out	How many are Left?	Put in	Put in	How many in all?
9	2	7	9	6	15
10	4	6	2	8	10
12	7	5	6	5	11
8	6	2	7	7	14
15	8	7	8	6	14

Page 24

1. Tuesday   2. Thursday
3. Monday   4. Saturday

Page 28

glad: happy, sad
noisy: loud, quiet
little: small, big
quick: fast, slow

Page 29

Animal names will vary.
Stories will vary. Make sure that
stories have two characters that
solve a problem.

Page 34

1. Ben
2. Anna
3. Mum
4. Dad

Page 35

1. fat
2. water
3. grass
4. hippo

Page 36

1. to the water fountain
2. flag
3. parrot
4. 2, 1, 3

5.

Page 37

5	10	6	22	13	8
11	15	7	18	31	14
17	20	25	32	47	71
36	22	30	35	40	48
51	56	43	33	45	50

Page 40

Page 38

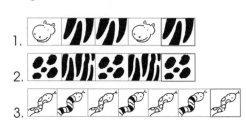

Page 39

Drawings will vary.

Page 41

The Stars of the Show

1. | 11 | 12 | 11 | 15 | 15 | 16 | 9 |
   | o | p | o | s | s | u | m |

2. | 4 | 5 | 5 | 14 |
   | d | e | e | r |

3. | 15 | 7 | 16 | 10 | 7 |
   | s | k | u | n | k |

4. | 15 | 13 | 16 | 6 | 14 | 14 | 5 | 8 |
   | s | q | u | i | r | r | e | l |

Riddles will vary.

Page 42

6:00   9:30   7:00

5:30   8:00   7:30

Page 43

1. B
2. E
3. A
4. D
5. C

Page 46

Page 44

Kinds of animals		Animals we want	Animals we have	How many more do we need?
camel		8	4	4
deer		15	9	6
giraffe		10	7	3
hippo		12	8	4
pig		14	7	7
sheep		18	9	9
buffalo		9	5	4
moose		13	6	7

Page 47

1. No
2. No
3. Yes
4. tracks
5. the forest
6. last night

Page 45

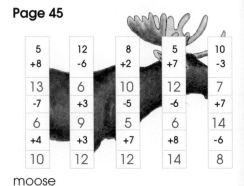

5	12	8	5	10
+8	-6	+2	+7	-3
13	6	10	12	7
-7	+3	-5	-6	+7
6	9	5	6	14
+4	+3	+7	+8	-6
10	12	12	14	8

moose

Page 48

2. 20¢, 20¢, 20¢, 10¢, 5¢ ; No
3. $1.00, 20¢, 10¢, 5¢, 5¢ ; Yes
4. $1.00, $1.00, $1.00, $1.00, $1.00 ; Yes

Answers

Page 49

1. $\begin{array}{r} 20\text{¢} \\ +75\text{¢} \\ \hline 95\text{¢} \end{array}$
2. $\begin{array}{r} 40\text{¢} \\ +50\text{¢} \\ \hline 90\text{¢} \end{array}$

3. $\begin{array}{r} 40\text{¢} \\ +35\text{¢} \\ \hline 75\text{¢} \end{array}$
4. $\begin{array}{r} 35\text{¢} \\ +50\text{¢} \\ \hline 85\text{¢} \end{array}$

Page 52

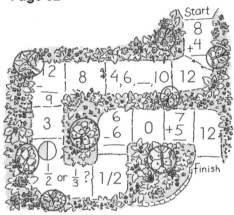

8 butterflies

Page 57

Reasons children like zoos will vary.

Page 50

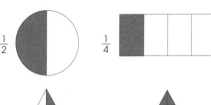

Page 53

Letters will vary but should follow correct letter form.

Pages 54–55

1. long tails
2. short tails
3. Bears' tails changed because Bear froze his tail in the pond and broke it off when he pulled it out of the ice.

Page 51

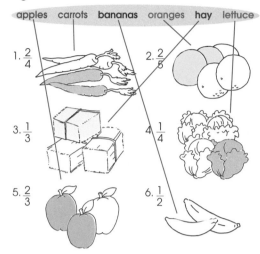

1. $\frac{2}{4}$ 2. $\frac{2}{5}$

3. $\frac{1}{3}$ 4. $\frac{1}{4}$

5. $\frac{2}{3}$ 6. $\frac{1}{2}$

Page 56

Guesses will vary. ▭

Answers

Answers

Page 62

S	T	W E N	W
B I L L Y			T
L	P E D R O		
K	C	D A N I	
G	J O S H		J

Page 63

swim
camp
fish
ride
hike
baseball
Answer will vary.

Page 64

Summer things:

beach towel   baseball cap
shorts   suitcase
picnic   swimsuit
beach ball   watermelon

Page 65

Names by houses in clockwise order:

Pedro

Billy

Wen

Page 66

4 additional players are needed.

Page 67

1. Pedro
2. Billy
3. Wen
4. Dani
5. Josh

Page 68

6 innings
Rockets

Page 69

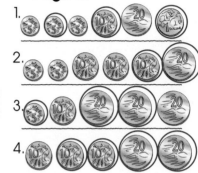

Page 70

4 Slippery Slide
3 Paddleboats
6 Wave Pool
2 Log Ride
5 Tube Trails
1 Beach
Answer will vary.

Page 71

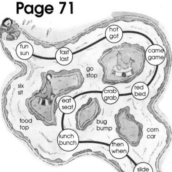

Page 72

1. in
2. cool
3. big
4. loud
5. fast
6. happy

Page 73

Answer will vary.

Pages 74–75

1. ghost town   4. coyote
2. no   5. pond
3. yes   Answer will vary.

Page 76

Page 77

Josh	Dani
$2.00	$3.00
60¢	40¢
10¢	30¢
10¢	5¢
$2.80	$3.75

Dani has saved more money.

Pages 78–79

1. Yes
2. Yes
3. No
4. No
5. Yes
6. Yes

Page 80

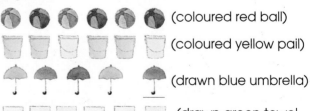
(coloured red ball)
(coloured yellow pail)
(drawn blue umbrella)
(drawn green towel with orange stripes)

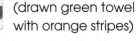
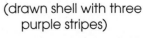
(drawn shell with three purple stripes)

Answers

Page 81

Living things:
crab
lifeguard
seagulls
shells (some shells are living)

Non-living things:
boat
flag
kite
shells

Page 82

Page 83

1. octopus
2. blowfish
3. hermit crab
4. sawfish
5. dolphin

Page 84

Coyote Desert
Black Bear Forest
Turtle Island
Giant Mountain

Page 85

1. cold
2. hot
3. dry
4. water
5. trees

Billy's family is going to Coyote Desert.

Page 86

1. bike
2. bus
3. car
4. jet
5. train

Page 87

Art and answers will vary. Look at the images to review art.

Pages 88–89

Postcard names from left to right:

Pedro, Dani and Josh, Billy, Wen

1. bear
2. ocean
3. calf
4. horse
5. desert

Page 90

Number of fish:
6, 10, 6, 4, 8

Page 91

Length of fish
(by 5¢ coins)
2
6
2
4
3
Estimations will vary but should be relatively close.

Page 92

Page 93

There are 13 insects.
Insect drawings will vary.

Page 94

They washed 4 dogs.

Page 95

1. Thursday
2. Sunday
3. Wednesday
4. Saturday

Page 96

1. 3
   Because it rained.
2. 8
   Because it was sunny.
3. Rainy days
Bonus: December

Page 97

1. 11
2. 8
3. 12
4. 6
5. 9
6. 5

Page 98

1. apples - 6
2. bananas - 7
3. carrots - 8
4. lettuce - 4
5. melons - 3
6. potatoes - 5

Page 99

1. apples
2. lettuce
3. bananas
4. apples
Check child's graph. Shaded areas should match the numbers found on page 98.

Page 100

1. 3 tens 2 ones 32
2. 4 tens 0 ones 40
3. 3 tens 2 ones 32
4. 5 tens 3 ones 53
5. 3 tens 0 ones 30
6. 3 tens 6 ones 36

	tens	ones
40	4	0
36	3	6

Page 101

Pedro picked 50 berries.
Billy picked 100 berries.

Page 102

Page 103

1. parade
2. Pedro
3. Drums
4. Bells
5. town

Page 104

1. Wen
2. holiday
3. 26 January
4. 2:00 P.M.
5. 123 Shady Lane
Answers will vary.

Page 105

1. brings milk
2. has bananas
3. takes a salad
4. carries hot dogs
5. eat together
Answers will vary.
Bonus Question: Pedro

Page 106

Let's watch!
Isn't this great?
Don't blink!
We're lucky!
I'm watching!

Page 107

1. 2:00
2. 10:00
3. 6:00
4. 11:00
5. 5:00

Pages 108–109 Totals include the participants.

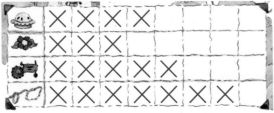

1. 6 people
2. 8 people
3. the roping contest
4. the flower show

Page 110

1. 2:00
   2:30
2. 5:00
   5:30
3. 7:00
   7:30
4. 8:00
5. 11:30
6. 3:00
7. 4:30

Page 111

Other coin variations acceptable.

Page 112

1. horse
2. pig
3. goat
4. cow
5. duck
6. dog

Page 113

Page 114

1. b
2. b
3. c
4. 2, 1, 4, 3

Page 115

1. 4, 4, 4
2. 3, 3, 0
3. 4, 4, 4
4. 4, 4, 2
5. 3, 3, 1
6. 5, 5, 2

Pages 116–117

1. Aisle 3, Row 3
2. Aisle 2, Row 2
3. Aisle 5, Row 1
4. Aisle 2, Row 4
5. Aisle 1, Row 3
6. Aisle 3, Row 5
7. Aisle 3, Row 1
8. Aisle 4, Row 4

Page 118

1. were
2. was
3. was
4. were
5. were

Page 119

1. did you have a nice summer?
2. name one thing you did.
3. will you take a trip next summer?
4. do you know where you will go?
5. i hope you have lots of fun.
6. Answer will vary.